Visiting a
SIKH TEMPLE

Visiting a
SIKH TEMPLE

Davinder Kaur Babraa

Photography
GAJINDER SINGH BABRAA

Design
JUDY BILLSON

LUTTERWORTH PRESS
CAMBRIDGE

Lutterworth Press
P.O. Box 60
Cambridge CB1 2NT

British Library Cataloguing in Publication Data available

Copyright © Davinder Kaur Babraa 1981

First published in UK 1981 by Lutterworth Press
Reprinted 1983, 1988

I would like to place on record my gratitude to the congregation of the
Woolwich Gurdwara, the President, Mr. Pritam Singh Matharu, members of
the Management Committee and Giani Bhagwant Singh for their support; to
the Rev. Philip Spence, Monica Spence, Miss Nita Panesar, Dr. Gobind Singh
Mansukhani, my husband Gajinder Singh Babraa, and my son Harpreet Singh
and many others who made helpful comments on the manuscript; to Mr. P.
S. Rani for providing information on Community Development Projects; Miss
Brenda McSkimming and my husband for typing the manuscript; and
especially to Miss Susan E. Tompkins for her help and encouragement.

ISBN 0-7188-2472-5

Additional photographs by Nick Lockett

Printed in Great Britain by
St Edmundsbury Press Limited, Bury St Edmunds, Suffolk

Contents

1. The Woolwich Gurdwara

Over the years many Sikhs have settled in the Woolwich area of south-east London. The Sikhs have a place of worship in Woolwich. It is called the Ramgarhia Community Centre.

This book is about this Centre which is popularly called the Woolwich Gurdwara. A **gurdwara** (or temple) is a place where Sikhs meet to worship God. Gurdwara is a **Punjabi** word and it means House of God*. Sikhs believe that there is one God and that he is the creator of this world and is present everywhere. Besides worship, other activities take place at the gurdwara, for this is the centre of the social and religious life of Sikhs.

The Sikh religion is one of the youngest of the world religions. It was founded in the Punjab in India in the late 15th century by Guru Nanak. **Guru** is an Indian word for a religious teacher, but when you hear Sikhs talking about a Guru, they mean one of the ten Sikh Gurus on whose teachings the Sikh religion is based.

When there were only a few Sikhs living in Woolwich, they used to hold their prayers and other religious activities every Sunday in an old church hall. As the number of Sikhs grew they felt the need to have a permanent place of worship. So they bought a public house in 1969, and converted it into a gurdwara. Soon this building proved too small for the Sikh religious activities in the area, so they started looking for another suitable place.

After a lot of searching, they found a fairly big building at Masons Hill, Woolwich. They bought this building in 1970 to convert it into a permanent Sikh Temple. The building was ideal because it had two large halls, a large kitchen, and several other small rooms. Each of these rooms is fully used as you will read later.

When the Sikhs bought this building it was in a poor state. During the war it had been badly damaged by bombs. After the war it was used for some time as a working-men's club. The men found it very difficult to maintain such a large building as

*Many Punjabi words are used in this book. Use the glossary at the end of the book to remind yourself of their meaning.

Some work still needs to be done on the outside of the building.

a social club so it was closed down in the early sixties.

Now once again this building is full of people, though they are there for a different purpose. Most of the rooms inside have been renovated and improved. Much more still needs to be done on the outside. Once all the work is finished, the building at Masons Hill will look as good as new.

2. Who are the Sikhs?

MIGRATION

The Sikhs who have settled in Woolwich originally came from the Punjab in Northern India. There are over ten million Sikhs in the world and most of them live in the State of Punjab. They are also found in other parts of India as well as in East Africa, Iran, Afghanistan, Malaysia, Singapore, the Philippines, Canada, the United States and Britain.

Sikhs began to come to Britain early in this century. Some came as students, and others to look for opportunities to set up businesses. It was only after the second world war that they came in large numbers to Britain as work was easily available then. The Sikhs started settling down in various parts of the country. Today most of the Asians in Southall are Sikhs, and many live in Leeds and other cities. Some Sikhs have also come from East Africa to live here. Get a map of the world and mark on it places where Sikhs are found today.

Many Sikhs own businesses and different kinds of shops.

WORK

Sikh men and women, living in Woolwich, earn their living by doing all kinds of work. You can see men driving buses and trains, while others work in the building industry as architects, builders, engineers and labourers. There are men and women doctors, surgeons, nurses, dentists, and opticians. Some Sikhs teach in schools in and around Woolwich, and others lecture in colleges. Some also work in the Civil Service. There are solicitors and lawyers too. Many men do skilled or semi-skilled jobs in factories. Others own businesses and sell all kinds of goods in their shops, whilst others trade in Indian foodstuffs. Many women help their husbands in shops, whilst others work as machinists at home or in the clothing factories.

DRESS

If you came to visit the Woolwich Gurdwara you would see men and women and boys and girls, wearing different styles of clothes. Men and boys will be seen in **turbans**. These are worn in various styles and colours. A turban is not merely a head-dress, but is directly connected with the Sikh way of life. It also shows that the wearer is a member of the Sikh community. A male Sikh makes a knot with his long hair on the top of his head and his turban covers this. It must reflect smartness, grace, and dignity.

Boys start wearing turbans at the age of about seven. A boy's first turban is tied on his head by a **granthi**, (a man who looks after the Sikh holy book), or an elderly person from the Sikh community. This is done in the presence of the holy book, and the boy's family and friends are also there. Boys quickly learn from their parents or older brothers or sisters how to tie and wear a turban.

The hair of a small boy is kept in place by plaiting it. When he is a little older his hair is made into a knot and covered with a square piece of cloth, called **patka**, the size of a man's handkerchief. Both the patka and the turban are made from plain or printed muslin, a very light weight cotton fabric. A turban is usually five metres long and about one metre wide. The turban for younger boys is shorter in length and width. Turbans are slightly starched every time they are washed to make them crisp, although elderly men prefer to wear them without starching.

6

Boys keep their hair tidy in different ways but men always wear turbans and many also like to wear traditional Indian clothes.

The rest of the clothing of a male Sikh is usually western. At the Gurdwara you will also see men wearing Indian clothes. These are usually a pair of **churidar pyjamas** (tight fitting trousers), and a **kurta** (a loose over-shirt). **Achkan**, a well fitted knee length tailored top, worn with churidar pyjamas is another favourite with men.

Women, as you would notice, wear more traditional Indian clothes. They normally dress in **salwar** and **kameeze**. This is a regional dress of the Punjab. Salwar is a specially designed pair of trousers and kameeze is the top, usually knee length. Sometimes instead of a salwar they may wear churidar pyjamas. **Dupatta** is worn with this dress. Dupatta is like a scarf worn around the shoulders or over the head. It is two metres long and about one metre wide. It is made of material which is very light in weight such as muslin, georgette or chiffon to match the rest of the clothes. The sari is another dress that women wear. In Britain and other western countries, girls and younger Sikh women tend to wear the western styled trousers and tops.

Before entering the prayer room of any gurdwara women and girls must cover their heads, no matter what their hair style. At

Sikh women like to wear traditional Indian clothes.

The Granth Sahib is written in Punjabi from left to right.

the Woolwich Gurdwara a notice about this is displayed near the entrance to the prayer room. Non Sikh visitors and any boys or men who have chosen not to wear turbans are also expected to cover their heads before entering the prayer room. They do this with a scarf or a man's handkerchief.

Younger boys and girls, many of them born in this country, are dressed very much like British boys and girls.

LANGUAGE

The whole of the worship at the Woolwich Gurdwara is held in Punjabi, the language the Sikhs speak. Services are always conducted in Punjabi, in all the gurdwaras of the world. The Punjabi language is also spoken by Hindus and Muslims living in the Punjab. The written script of the Punjabi language is called **Gurmukhi**. The word itself means 'from the mouth of the Guru'. It came to be known as Gurmukhi because the alphabet, containing thirty five letters, was introduced by Guru Angad Dev, the second Guru of the Sikhs. It is written from left to right. The entire **Guru Granth Sahib**, the holy book of the Sikhs, is written in Gurmukhi. Find out all you can about the Gurmukhi alphabet. Are any of the sounds the same as English letters?

9

3. The outside of the Gurdwara

There are many gurdwaras in England. In fact wherever you see a community of Sikhs you will probably also find a gurdwara there. The gurdwara at Woolwich was founded by the Sikhs to meet their religious and social needs. As it is expensive to erect new buildings, the Sikhs in England buy a disused church or any other suitable building and convert it into a gurdwara. For any building to be called a gurdwara it must have the Granth Sahib, also called **Adi Granth**, placed in the building as described in chapter 4. Usually the largest room in the building is used for this purpose.

The Sikhs in Woolwich are very proud of their gurdwara, especially because they carried out the improvement of the building themselves. The money for this came from Sikhs, who made very generous donations, sometimes of their unopened pay packets. Those who could not afford to give money offered their skills and their time. Sikhs have not asked anybody else for any money for the improvement of the gurdwara building. A Sikh never begs.

ARCHITECTURE

The gurdwara building at Woolwich has a dome at the top which makes it look very much like a gurdwara in India. The dome makes the building look more beautiful and majestic. The two large halls at the Woolwich Gurdwara have several plain glass windows on either side which keep the rooms bright and sunny. In India the windows of gurdwaras are often made of stained glass with decorative or pictorial designs. The outside is usually finished in white, as this represents purity and also allows the building to be seen from a distance.

THE FLAG

The Woolwich Gurdwara stands out amongst other buildings around it, not only because of its size, but also because of the Sikh flag which flies high over the dome. The Sikhs call their flag **Nishan Sahib**. The flag is a very important outside feature of any

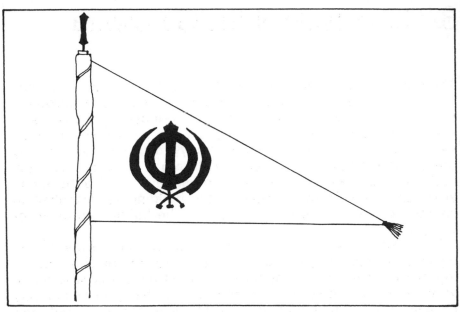

The Sikh flag flies from the top of the gurdwara all the time.

The Golden Temple in India is the most famous Sikh gurdwara.

gurdwara, as it shows that the building belongs to the Sikh community.

The flag is triangular in shape and is yellowish-orange in colour. It remains at full mast throughout the year on a tall flag pole which is also draped in cloth similar to the flag. The pointed end of the flag is finished with a tassle. A new flag is flown every year in April with great affection and enthusiasm. April is the month in which Sikhs celebrate their New Year. The Sikhs may bow to the flag and wherever possible touch the base of the flag pole with their foreheads before entering a gurdwara. This is not possible at Woolwich because the flag pole is not at ground level.

In the middle of the flag is the sign of the Sikhs, which is called **khanda**. This is made from black material. The two-edged sword in the centre represents freedom and justice. A Sikh is taught to defend his honour and to be fair in his dealings with everyone in every way. There are two more swords, one on either side of the two-edged sword. The sword on the right marks guidance in religious matters, and the one on the left guidance in worldly matters. The circle in the middle, called **chakkar**, emphasizes the balance between these two. It has other meanings also such as that all people in this world are equal.

THE GOLDEN TEMPLE

Many of the gurdwaras in India and Pakistan mark historic sites. One such has become world famous. It is the Golden Temple in Amritsar. The Sikhs call it Harmandir Sahib or the House of the Lord. Most Sikh children in Woolwich will have seen pictures of the Golden Temple and have heard from their parents that it is a wonderful place. Few have actually visited it. You can find out from other books about the Golden Temple and other historic gurdwaras.

Men and women sit separately on the floor for worship.

4. Inside Woolwich Gurdwara

The Woolwich Gurdwara is the biggest Sikh temple in Britain south of the river Thames. It is used for worship and for social functions like marriages and other ceremonies. Up to three thousand people have been known to visit the gurdwara for Sikh festivals.

There are two large halls in this building. The one next to the kitchen is used as a dining hall and for other purposes. The other one is used for worship. There is an office for the Management Committee, a library, store rooms and a room for the Community Development Officer and residence of the granthi within the main building.

Apart from the prayer hall and other rooms, the Gurdwara has rest rooms where any traveller can stop to rest for a day or more free of charge. All gurdwaras provide rest rooms, cloakrooms, bathrooms and toilet facilities.

Besides being a place of worship, this Gurdwara is used as a place where Sikhs meet to discuss matters which are important to their lives. The rooms in the building also serve as a school for children to learn about Sikhism. With such activities going on in the Gurdwara it has become very much a part of the Sikh community in the Woolwich area.

THE PRAYER ROOM

This is an important room in any gurdwara. At the Woolwich Gurdwara along the walls you will see pictures of Gurus and of incidents depicting their lives, but they are not the objects of worship. The floor is carpeted and covered with large white sheets, on which the congregation sit, often cross-legged. A narrow strip of carpet leads from the middle of the entrance door to the Granth Sahib. This divides the room into two sections. Men and women sit separately in each section but worship together. Children usually stay with their mothers.

The most striking feature of the prayer room is the Guru Granth Sahib. This is placed on a platform under a richly decorated wooden canopy which stands on a dais, a low platform across

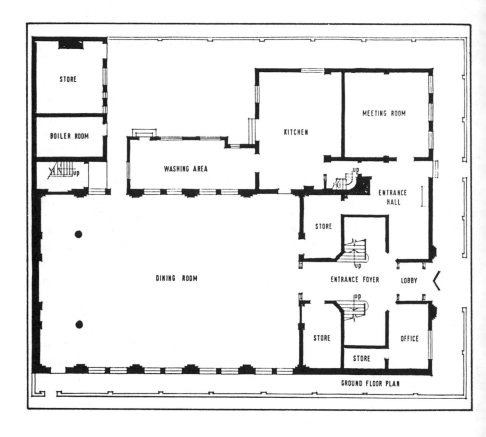

the end of the room. In some gurdwaras, in place of a canopy, you would see a **chanani**. This is a large square piece of cloth, the sides of which are finished with a heavily gathered or pleated frill, or sometimes a fringe. The Granth Sahib is treated with great reverence, and therefore it is kept higher than the place where people sit.

On the platform of the canopy is placed a miniature bed, called **Manji Sahib**. This is completely covered with a soft quilt. Over this are placed two white cloths. On these are placed three small cushions, on top of which rests the Granth Sahib. As the Granth Sahib is a very large book, the cushions help to support it and tilt it so that the reader can see the writing more clearly.

The platform is covered with a cloth. The Granth Sahib itself is covered with a separate cloth, called a **rumala** which usually

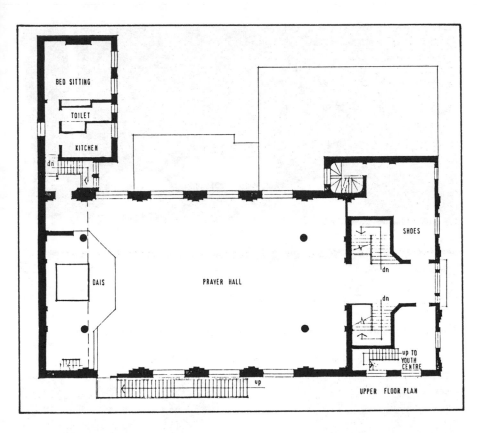

Within the floor plan:

BED SITTING

TOILET

KITCHEN

dn

SHOES

dn

DAIS

PRAYER HALL

dn

UP TO
YOUTH
CENTRE

up

UPPER FLOOR PLAN

matches the other cloths. The edges of these cloths are usually finished with a trimming. A rumala, donated from time to time by members of the congregation, is used to cover the Granth Sahib as a token of respect. The rumala also protects the Granth Sahib from getting dirty. The space in front of the Manji Sahib is covered with an attractive rug and decorated with fresh flowers.

On the other side of the Granth Sahib is kept a **chaur**. This is like a fly-whisk and is made of yak hair embedded in a wooden or silver handle. When the granthi or any other reader, man or woman, sits behind the Granth Sahib waiting to read it, he will wave the chaur over it. When the Granth Sahib is being read, then an attendant stands behind the reader to wave the chaur. The waving of a chaur is a sign of respect for the Granth Sahib.

The Granth Sahib is supported by three cushions on the Manji Sahib.

A chaur is waved over the Granth Sahib to show respect.

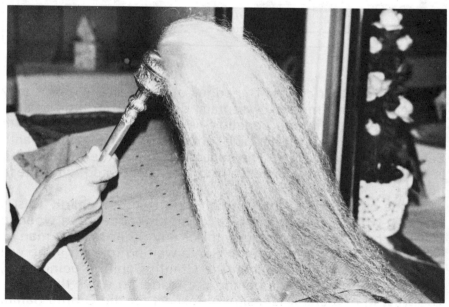

When people come into the building they remove their shoes outside the prayer room, and give them to the shoekeeper. With heads covered people walk to the Granth Sahib and place their offerings of money and food on the rug before kneeling down to bow and touch the forehead to the floor. At the Woolwich Gurdwara the offering of the money is placed in a large metal safe through a slit in its lid. At the end of the service the money is counted by the treasurer. Food such as milk, sugar, butter, flour, fruit etc., may be brought as an offering. This is sent down to the kitchens straight away. It is not compulsory to give money or food as an offering.

GURU GRANTH SAHIB

The Granth Sahib contains **Gurbani**, the Word of the Gurus. It includes the work of the first five and the ninth Gurus as well as of holy saints who were not themselves Sikhs. Gurbani is written in verse and all the poems and songs are set to Indian classical or folk music.

The first copy of the Granth Sahib was compiled by Guru Arjan, the fifth Guru, in 1604 and was handwritten under his direction. This copy now exists in Kartarpur in the Punjab. Guru Gobind Singh, the tenth Guru, added the hymns of his father, the ninth Guru, to the Granth Sahib. In 1708, before his death, he declared an end to the line of the Sikh Gurus and transferred all the functions of the Guru to his followers and the Granth Sahib; thus the term Guru Granth Sahib. This is why all Sikhs now treat their holy book as their Guru.

Granth Sahib is a large book containing 1,430 pages and 5,894 hymns and verses. Every copy of the Granth Sahib is identical. It is written in bold Gurmukhi print and each chapter starts with the **Mool Mantra**. These words are Guru Nanak's description of God. The words say that there is only one God and his name is Truth. His spirit is everywhere. He is the creator of the universe, and he himself does not die or take birth. He does not fear anyone nor has he any enemies. He is timeless and formless.

The Granth Sahib teaches that all people are born equal. It teaches Sikhs to live a life free of rituals and superstitions. To find God you should do good and serve people round you and not keep yourself aloof. It stresses the importance of family life. All Sikh Gurus were married, except the eighth Guru who died

Worshippers bow in front of the Granth Sahib.

as a young boy. In the Granth Sahib the Gurus emphasized that Sikhs should gather together for worship and meditation, seek good company, serve the community, and work for the good of all.

Sikhs consider themselves very privileged to have a direct record of the original words of the Gurus in the form of the Granth Sahib. Not a single word has been altered, added or removed since its preparation. To the Sikhs the Granth Sahib is the greatest treasure. They seek its guidance on every possible occasion and no ceremony in the Sikh way of life is complete unless conducted in its presence. Arrange a visit to your nearest gurdwara and find out how Sikhs conduct their service.

THE KITCHEN

The kitchen at the Woolwich Gurdwara is fitted with specially designed gas cookers and stainless steel working surfaces in order to prepare the food in the most hygienic conditions. The kitchen is well stocked with large pans and pots required for cooking Punjabi food.

An additional room for washing-up has been built next to the kitchen with two connecting openings to the dining hall. This enables all the dirty dishes to be returned to the washing-up area without going through the kitchen.

THE DINING HALL

The dining hall is the same size as the prayer room. It is used for eating as well as for other activities such as indoor games and the showing of educational or historical films to the Sikhs and their friends. People sit on rugs on the floor to eat. Alcoholic drinks and food containing meat, fish and eggs must not be served in the gurdwaras. Smoking is completely forbidden for the Sikhs and a notice about this has been put up in the entrance hall so that any non-Sikh visitors also refrain from smoking.

Sikhs living in the Woolwich area use this hall and the cooking facilities for wedding receptions. The Gurdwara is well stocked with tables and chairs which are used for social events.

Early every morning the Granth Sahib is carried downstairs.

Singing the hymns of the Gurus is an important part of worship.

5. Services of worship

There is no fixed day for worship for Sikhs but at Woolwich the main service of the week is held on Sunday evenings. On Sunday everybody is free to come to the Gurdwara. Besides worshipping, the congregation may receive religious instruction from respected members of the community or from a granthi or a giani, and also discuss matters of community concern.

GRANTHI

At Woolwich Gurdwara there are two granthis. A **granthi** is an important person and is directly concerned with the day to day religious affairs of the gurdwara. A granthi not only looks after the Granth Sahib but is also skilled in reciting the Sikh scriptures and the daily prayers. In small gurdwaras he also acts as a caretaker, but at Woolwich they have a separate caretaker.

GIANI

The assistant granthi at Woolwich is also a **giani**. A giani is a scholar of Punjabi language and literature. He or she is a very respected and sought-after person in a Sikh community. This is because he can explain clearly and simply the meaning of the Sikh scriptures which are written in poetry. It is the poetic language which many find difficult to understand.

Present-day gianis, who are deeply concerned about their religion, do further training in the study of scripture and of other religions. The giani at Woolwich has done further training of this kind.

A giani or a granthi does not have to wear any kind of uniform or special clothes. However, they prefer to wear the Indian clothes. These are worn for many reasons. One is to keep the style of dress that was used by the Sikh Gurus, particularly Guru Gobind Singh. Another reason for wearing this dress is that it is in keeping with the Punjabi way of dressing and tradition.

THE SUNDAY SERVICE

Every Sunday, in the earlier part of the evening, Sikhs from

Woolwich and the neighbourhood, make their way to the Gurdwara. Usually all the family attend the service together. The service lasts about two hours and quite a large number of people go.

Just before the service begins, the granthi takes his place behind the Granth Sahib. The service begins with the giani reciting the evening prayer. After this prayer there is singing of hymns from the scriptures. This is accompanied by drums and sometimes other instruments. The Gurus encouraged singing. Many Sikhs will tell you that if you listen to this singing with rapt attention and in a meditative mood, you can experience contentment and peace of mind.

Besides singing, religious or historical poetry may be read, and speeches may be given by adults or children from the congregation. The Sunday service may consist only of singing by the local or visiting musicians or may include other items in the programme. People who participate in these activities feel that this is one way in which they can serve God and fellow Sikhs. The giani usually gives a sermon, or talk, lasting fifteen to twenty minutes. During this sermon he may explain to the congregation some verses of the Granth Sahib or help them to understand how they as Sikhs should live their daily life. He may preach about the work of Sikh Gurus or of a Sikh saint the anniversary of whose birth or death happens to fall in that week. Children are encouraged to take part in hymn singing and telling stories from the lives of Gurus and are often rewarded with small presents to keep up their enthusiasm.

In the last part of the service, the secretary thanks all those who have taken part, including the congregation without whom the service would not be possible. He also gives details of forthcoming events. After this the seated congregation recite **Anand Sahib**, a hymn of joy. Anand Sahib is always recited at any service or religious ceremony except a funeral. At the end of this hymn, all stand with their hands folded together in front of them, heads slightly bowed and sing the first part of the prayer in the praise of God.

The next part of the prayer called **Ardas** is offered by the giani, the granthi or by any other baptised Sikh (see chapter 6), while the congregation remain silent. Here the congregation is reminded of the teachings of the Gurus, the sufferings and sacrifices of the Sikh martyrs, and the words of the Guru Granth Sahib. At this point all bow down to the floor and stand up again to recite the final part of the Ardas where God is asked to keep the **Khalsa** faithful and to bless the whole of mankind. (The term Khalsa is used for the baptised Sikhs. It means 'pure ones.') All bow down once again and then sit down. At this point the giani or the granthi opens the Granth Sahib at random and reads a brief verse from the left-hand side of the page to the congregation. The meaning of this reading is explained to the congregation by the giani. This is the end of the service.

KARAH PARSHAD

After the service **Karah Parshad** is served in small amounts to the congregation. You must always take it with your two hands cupped together, and eat it straight away. Karah Parshad is made from semolina, clarified butter, sugar and water. It can be made by men or women. They must bathe first and put on clean clothes. They should also make sure that the utensils to be used, the stove and the kitchen are also clean. They must remove their shoes outside the kitchen, and then start preparing the Parshad.

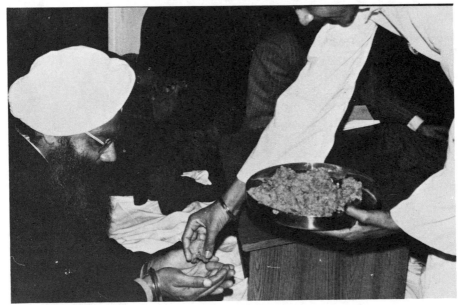

Eating Karah Parshad together shows fellowship and equality.

To make Parshad they first cook semolina in butter in a large pan until golden brown. They then add syrup made from the sugar and water and continue to cook the mixture until it binds together and becomes thick. During the preparation they must recite hymns from the Granth Sahib. When the Parshad is cooked it is covered with a clean white cloth. One of the volunteers carries water in a clean container and sprinkles it, to symbolise cleanliness, all the way to the prayer room in front of the person carrying the Parshad. The Parshad is placed on a table near the Granth Sahib. During the Ardas the Parshad is marked by a sword as a way of blessing it. So when you are given Parshad you must not waste it. Parshad is an expression of equality and unity within the Sikh community. It is also a symbol of common brotherhood of the people of the world.

LANGAR

After the congregation have eaten Parshad, they may get together for a friendly talk and go to the dining hall to eat food called **Guru ka Langar**. You have to take off your shoes outside the dining hall before sitting down to eat. Langar is the food cooked

Different families take turns to provide and cook Langar.

The meal is provided free for everyone.

in the gurdwara's community kitchen. Anyone who wishes to pay for Langar must tell the secretary of the Management Committee of the Gurdwara in advance so that his name can be put on the list. Paying for the Langar, cooking and serving it, is considered one of the greatest acts of charity. You may have to wait several weeks before your turn for providing Langar comes.

When everybody sits down, people of all ages first give out special stainless steel plates and spoons and then bring the food round to serve. You can always have more food if you wish as the servers move round with the food until everybody has eaten. People must eat all the food they take as the food is always blessed before it is served. For this reason it is considered unholy to waste food on your plate. Everybody is expected to eat the same food, no matter who has paid for it or cooked it. Langar breaks down any differences among people and gives them an opportunity to do service for others. Like Karah Parshad, Langar symbolises unity among the Sikhs, equality and common brotherhood of man.

Every night the Granth Sahib is put to rest.

PUTTING THE GRANTH SAHIB TO REST

One of the last duties of the granthi before going to bed is to recite the night prayer (**Kirtan Sohilla**,) and then put the Granth Sahib to rest. On Sunday evenings it is done soon after the distribution of the Karah Parshad. To do this, the rumala and the two side cloths from the Granth Sahib are removed. The Granth Sahib is then closed and neatly wrapped in the two white cloths under the three small cushions, as mentioned in chapter 4. The Granth Sahib is then carried on the granthi's head to the room above the canopy. It stays there all night on a Manji Sahib under a rumala and is brought down again in the morning. Whenever the Granth Sahib is taken away or brought back all present must stand as an act of respect. The steps leading to this room are on the left side of the dais. Extra copies of the Granth Sahib and spare rumalas are also kept in this room.

WEEKDAY ACTIVITY

Sometimes on a weekday evening visiting musicians sing hymns

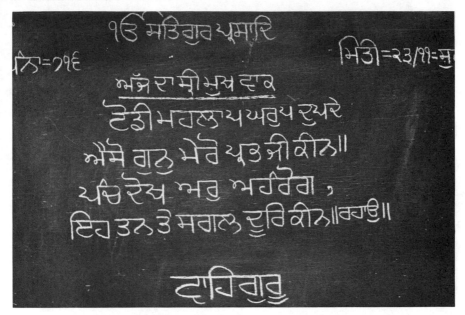

The Hukamnamah for the day is shown on a notice board.

and religious songs. Up to a hundred or more people can be seen at these performances.

Every day in the early hours of the morning, before dawn, the morning prayer, **Japji Sahib**, is recited to start the day. This is the time when the Granth Sahib is brought back into the prayer room where it stays until night time. After the Granth Sahib is properly placed it is opened at random and the first complete verse on the left hand page is read. This random reading from any page is called **Vak** or **Hukamnamah** and serves as a lesson or thought for the day. The wordings of the Vak are displayed on the notice board in the hallway of the gurdwara. Anyone who is able to read Gurmukhi can come and read the Granth Sahib during the day. Some people come to say their own private prayers.

In the evening at about sunset, the evening prayer is read to end the day. Finally at night Kirtan Sohilla is recited and the Granth Sahib put to rest. At the end of each of three prayers, Ardas is always offered and Karah Parshad served to anyone who may be present at the time.

The entire Granth Sahib is read before every festival.

Every year the flag pole is cleaned and draped in yellow cloth.

6. Festivals and ceremonies

Sikhs call their festivals **gurpurbs**. As the Sikhs celebrate their festivals by the lunar calendar (that is, based on the phases of the moon), the dates are not the same every year. A calendar giving the details and dates of all the festivals is available at the gurdwara. In Britain it is not convenient to celebrate the festival on a working day, so it is celebrated on the nearest Sunday to the actual date.

With the help of the two granthis, the Management Committee of the Woolwich Gurdwara decide on the date of the celebration of a particular festival and announce it beforehand to the congregation. It also goes on the notice-board. When the Committee has worked out the details for the festival, it publishes and distributes leaflets giving the complete programme. This is done about two weeks before the festival. The important festivals are Baisakhi and the birthday anniversaries of Guru Nanak and Guru Gobind Singh, and the martyrdom of Guru Arjan and Guru Teg Bahadhur. You can find out more about the Gurus from other books.

The celebration of any festival starts with the **Akhand Path**. This is a continuous reading of the entire Guru Granth Sahib by readers, men or women, done in relays of one or two hours. The readers must give their names a few days earlier to the granthi who then makes a timetable for them to follow. It takes forty-eight hours to complete the reading which starts early in the morning two days before the gurpurb. Each reader must have a bath and dress in clean clothes to do his turn of reading in the Akhand Path.

As many people as can come early in the morning of the festival day to listen to the reading of the last five pages of the Granth Sahib. This concludes the Akhand Path. It is followed by the usual prayers, readings and hymns, and Karah Parshad is distributed. The rest of the programme is very much like that on Sunday evenings, with participants getting more time for their activities. All the singing, preaching, sermons, poetry etc., is about the life of the Guru in whose honour the festival is celebrated. The Woolwich Gurdwara gets very full on such mornings. In India processions go through the streets and the Granth Sahib is carried on a float.

BAISAKHI

Baisakhi is celebrated on 13th April each year. It is also a new year day in the Punjab as well as the beginning of the harvest season. To the Sikhs this is a day of great importance. They celebrate the anniversary of the birth of the Khalsa. Baisakhi is celebrated by holding Akhand Path as for the other festivals. On this day the year-old flag is brought down and the new one hoisted. At Woolwich the flag ceremony takes place before mid-morning.

This is also a time when new members are initiated into the Khalsa brotherhood. Sikhs prefer this period for initiation, because the first ceremony of initiation was performed during Baisakhi by Guru Gobind Singh in 1699. However, initiation can take place any time during the year. The assembling of Sikhs to worship God and to listen to the teachings of the Guru at Baisakhi was originally started by Guru Amardas, the third Guru, more than four hundred years ago.

There are certain ceremonies which have become part of the Sikh way of life.

INITIATION

The initiation ceremony, known as **Amrit Parchar**, is held once every year at Woolwich Gurdwara. At other times all gurdwaras in London get together and have the ceremony in one place. Notice about the forthcoming initiation ceremony is given to the congregation several months beforehand. This is so that those who wish to be initiated can prepare for the event. Sikhs believe that the initiation ceremony completely changes a person's life, so that from then on they live a new and blessed life.

Who is eligible for the initiation?

1. Any person, man or woman, about sixteen years or over is eligible. You can belong to any religion, race and nationality. It also does not matter what language you speak. The important point is that you are willing to change and that you fully understand the Sikh Code of Conduct and Discipline.

32

2. You should be able to read the Sikh prayers and understand their meaning.
3. Sikh children under the age of sixteen can be initiated if their parents take full responsibility to see that they follow and keep the Code.
4. If you are not a Sikh, you have to undergo some training to ensure that you understand and can follow the Sikh Code of Conduct. It is essential that you give up smoking and drinking.

The ceremony is always performed in the presence of the Granth Sahib. This is usually in a gurdwara, but if any other place is to be used then the Granth Sahib must be installed there. The ceremony is conducted by five men who are themselves baptised, or initiated and observe the Sikh Code of Conduct and Discipline. The five men are called **Panj Pyare**, the Five Beloved Sikhs.

Using five Sikhs to adminster the baptism goes back to the time of Guru Gobind Singh and the Baisakhi festival of 1699. On this Baisakhi day many thousands of people gathered to listen to the Guru and to receive his blessings. When the Guru appeared before the congregation he was carrying a sword. He made an alarming demand of his people. He wanted the head of a Sikh who considered himself a real follower of the Guru. One man stood up and offered his head. He was taken by the Guru into a tent nearby. The Guru returned with his sword dripping with blood and repeated his call for another head. When he had got five men in this manner he returned once more, this time with the five men alive and unharmed, dressed just like himself.

On seeing this breathtaking spectacle the congregation was convinced that the Guru had performed a miracle by bringing the five back to life. He announced to the congregation, 'These are my Five Beloved Elect. Their spirit shall be part of my body and spirit, and mine shall be theirs.' These men who had passed the toughest of tests, were then baptised by Guru Gobind Singh. He asked them to baptise him in the same way as he had done to them. These five men were the beginning of the Khalsa Brotherhood. The Panj Pyare today baptise people in the same way as it was done by Guru Gobind Singh.

The Five Ks

Persons to be initiated into the Khalsa Brotherhood should on the day of initiation bathe, wash their hair, and dress in absolutely clean clothes. They should also be in possession of five symbols, all starting with the letter K. Men and women wear the same symbols as in Sikh religion both the sexes enjoy equal rights.

1. **Kes** This is the uncut hair on the head and face. The hair on the head of a man must be covered with a turban and that of a woman with a dupatta. A Sikh must not remove any hair from any part of his body.
2. **Kanga** This is a small comb. It is for keeping the hair clean and tidy. Kanga is usually made of wood or ivory. It can be made from other materials such as plastic.
3. **Kirpan** This is a sword made from steel, and is usually eight to ten inches long. Kirpan signifies honour, dignity, bravery and self sacrifice. It reminds the wearer of his duty to defend the weak and uphold the truth.
4. **Kara** This is an all steel bracelet. It is not worn as an ornament. Kara is worn on the right wrist reminding the wearer

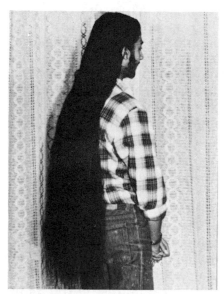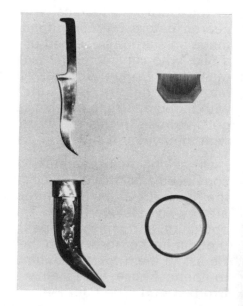

Four of the Five Ks.

of his unity with God and the Khalsa Brotherhood.
5. **Kach** A Kach is a pair of shorts worn as underwear. All baptised Sikhs, men and women, wear them. They used to be knee length when they were originally introduced by the Guru, to replace other forms of dress such as dhoti which did not allow freedom of movement in battle.

The Ceremony

The only people present at the ceremony are the persons to be initiated, the Panj Pyare and the granthi. As this is a solemn occasion and one to be conducted with complete concentration, family, friends and other members of the congregation are generally not allowed to be present. The principles of the Sikh faith are explained to the new members. When they vow to live the Sikh faith and follow the teachings of the Gurus, Ardas is offered. The Panj Pyare, dressed in blue turbans and yellow tunics and with a blue sash over the shoulder and round the waist, prepare the **amrit**, the baptismal water. To do so **patasas**, a kind of puffed sugar cake, are stirred in fresh water in a steel bowl with the double-edged steel sword, the type you see on the Sikh flag. Five different prayers are said during the preparation. The Panj Pyare must sit round the steel bowl in a circle resting on the right knee with both hands on the edge of the bowl. This position keeps a person on the alert and ready to take action when needed. Water is used because it is the source of life, it purifies and cleans the body and brings back freshness. Also when water has been blessed with the prayers it cleanses the soul. When Guru Gobind Singh prepared the amrit, his wife had put the sugar cakes into the water, denoting that the amrit was to be as much a drink of religious importance for women as for men. By doing so she not only added sweetness but also feminine grace, tenderness and compassion. The use of a steel bowl and sword depicts unshakeable strength and firmness.

The person being initiated drinks the amrit five times from his cupped hands, has it sprinkled five times into his eyes and five times into his hair. Each time he receives amrit, he has to say, *Waheguru ji ka khalsa, Waheguru ji ki Fateh*, meaning, 'The Khalsa is dedicated to God, Victory ever is of Almighty Lord!' These words are also used when any Sikh begins and finishes his address to the congregation in a gurdwara. It was at this cer-

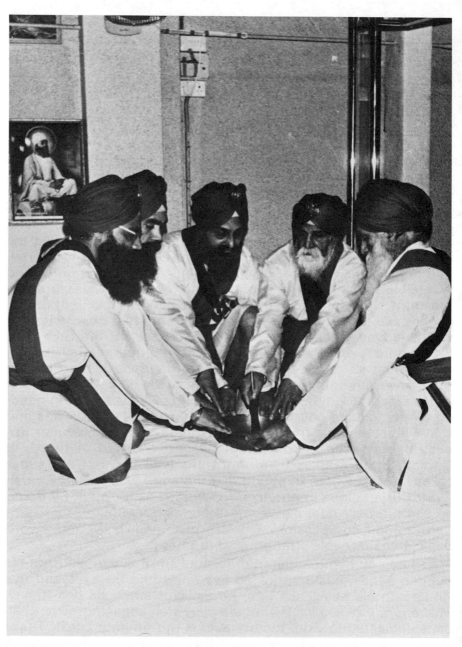

The baptismal water, or amrit, is prepared by the Panj Pyare.

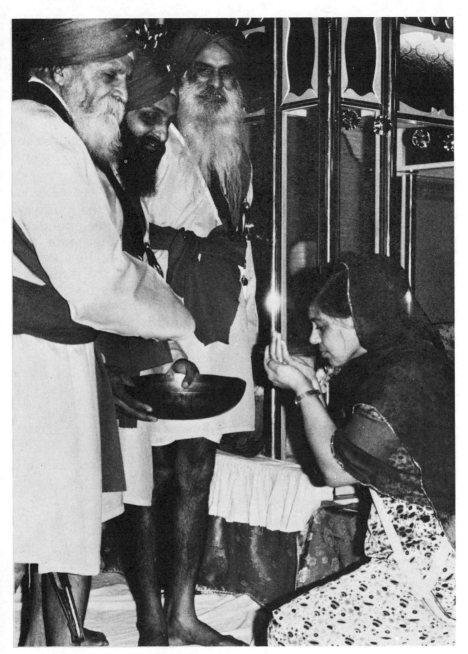

The person being initiated drinks the amrit five times.

emony that Guru Gobind Singh introduced the word **Singh** meaning lion at the end of male names, and **Kaur** meaning princess at the end of female names. He himself changed his name from Gobind Rai to Gobind Singh, and his wife Sahib Devi to Sahib Kaur. The initiation ceremony ends with the reading of Anand Sahib, the offering of Ardas followed by Vak. Karah Parshad is served to all present. You may know a Sikh boy or girl who has recently been initiated. Ask him or her to describe the experience to you.

NAMING

When a baby is a few days old, he or she is taken to the gurdwara for blessing and name giving. Family and friends attend the ceremony. The granthi first prepares amrit and then puts it on the baby's tongue with the tip of a kirpan or khanda. He sprinkles some of it on the baby's face and head, and gives the remainder to the mother to drink. Amrit for this ceremony is prepared by one person, and only the first five verses of the Japji Sahib are recited during the preparation. The Granth Sahib is then opened at random. The parents decide on a name which must begin with

The granthi prepares amrit for the baby's blessing and name giving.

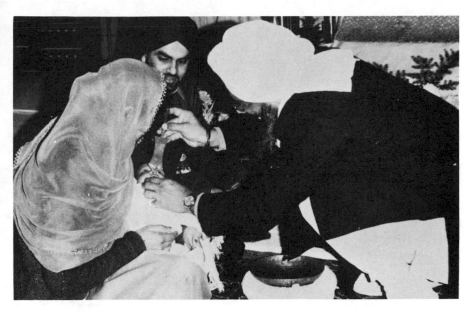

Amrit is put on the baby's tongue.

the first letter of the first word of the first verse on the left hand page. Singh or Kaur is then added, and the name announced publicly in the gurdwara. On this occasion parents normally pay for the Karah Parshad and also give, as an offering, a rumala for the Granth Sahib. The ceremony is completed by reading Anand Sahib, offering Ardas, taking Vak and distributing Karah Parshad.

MARRIAGE

Most couples get engaged before marriage but this is not absolutely necessary. All wedding arrangements are made by the bride's parents. A Sikh marriage can take place on any day early in the morning but here at Woolwich most marriages are arranged to take place on Saturdays and Sundays in the morning. These days are chosen as they are convenient for friends and relatives to come.

Marriage, performed according to the Sikh rites, in the presence of the Granth Sahib, is the only way of getting married which is acceptable to Sikhs. However, by law all Sikh marriages must also be recorded by the Registrar of Marriages. According to the Sikh faith a truly wedded couple would have one spirit in two bodies because in spiritual union complete happiness and

Sikh weddings are performed in the presence of the Granth Sahib and the couple walk round it four times.

satisfaction is found.

The bride and bridegroom sit in front of the Granth Sahib. The bride always sits on the left and the groom on the right. The bride is usually dressed in reds or pinks as these colours are worn on all happy occasions. The bridegroom's turban is usually pink. Before the marriage vows are read, the granthi asks the couple and their parents to stand for a short prayer in which he asks God almighty to bless the marriage. This is a way of giving public consent to the marriage. After this prayer, the musicians sing a hymn about marriage. The bride's father then makes her hold one end of a scarf, and the groom, on whose shoulders the scarf rests, holds the other end. The scarf is usually pink. The granthi then chants the first verse of the wedding song called **Lavan**. The musicians begin to sing the same verse. The couple, the bride following the groom, walk slowly in a clockwise direction round the Granth Sahib, still holding the scarf. They come back to their place as the verse comes to an end, bow to the Granth Sahib in confirmation of the vow and sit down. This process is repeated for the remaining three verses. On the fourth round flower petals and confetti may be showered over the cou-

The couple sign the Marriage Register.

ple to wish them all happiness. This is not allowed at Woolwich as it is not an essential custom.

The ceremony ends with the reading of Anand Sahib followed by Ardas. Vak is taken and Karah Parshad is served. After this the guests are entertained to refreshments in the gurdwara's dining hall, by the bride's parents. At the end of all this the bridegroom takes the bride away to live in his home.

DEATH

When a member of the Sikh community in Woolwich dies, the granthi is informed so that he may prepare for the funeral. Sikhs cremate their dead. Death is accepted as God's will and Sikhs come to the gurdwara to offer prayers for the deceased person.

Before the cremation, the dead body is bathed and dressed by the family making sure that it is wearing the five Sikh symbols. Ardas is said before removing the body from the house. At the crematorium, the granthi performs the last religious rites by reciting Kirtan Sohilla, the last prayer of the day. Relatives and friends join him in reciting. Ardas and special prayers for the soul's eternal peace are offered and the body is then cremated. All the family and friends attend the cremation. All of them go to the gurdwara from the crematorium, where the granthi reads a special passage about death from the Granth Sahib and finishes with Anand Sahib, Ardas and Vak. Karah Parshad is served to all.

At the home of the deceased the family arranges for a **Sehaj Path**. This is a reading of the Granth Sahib slowly with intervals in between. It takes ten days to read the entire Granth Sahib in this manner. This is the same length of time as the period of mourning. If the family is able to read they must take part in the reading. If some one else reads for them then they must sit and listen to the reading. The reason for doing so is to gain strength by remembering God during the sad period and to accept his will. If there is no room to keep the Granth Sahib at home, the Sehaj Path can be done in the gurdwara. The concluding ceremony of the Path takes place at the gurdwara in the late afternoon. The hymns sung at this time are about death. The family of the deceased may provide Langar. The method of cremating the dead in India is different from here in England. See if you can find out what the difference is.

7. The Gurdwara and the community

There are three things which are of great importance to Sikhs. They are work, worship, and charity. Doing service for the benefit of the community and one's fellow men is regarded as very important. The Sikhs who worship at the Woolwich Gurdwara have shown that they value this teaching of the Gurus. Sikhs can serve their fellow men in three different ways.

1. **With their hands** They can feed the hungry, care for the sick, sweep the gurdwara precincts, look after the shoes of the congregation, do any repair work in the gurdwara, cook, serve and wash up in the community kitchen.
2. **With their minds** They can teach Sikhs and others to read and write their language, and explain the text of the Granth Sahib and how the hymns are sung.
3. **With their money** Sikhs should keep apart one tenth of their income in the name of God, and use it for charity. Sikhs help people in need whatever their race or religion.

The rest of this chapter shows some of the ways in which the Sikhs at Woolwich follow this teaching.

THE MANAGEMENT COMMITTEE

The day to day running of the Woolwich Gurdwara is controlled by the Management Committee which consists of twenty two members. These members are democratically elected by the congregation. The Honorary President, two Vice Presidents, Secretary, Joint Secretary, Stage Secretary, Treasurer and Sub-Treasurer are elected every two years to serve the community. They work hard to make sure that worshippers are able to pray comfortably and to see that they can use the centre to meet together and discuss things of common interest and find solutions to their problems.

The Committee keeps the congregation informed of any government policies that are going to affect their life in Britain. Sometimes they have to consider delicate and touchy issues, especially those which interfere with their way of life. For instance at some places of work and some schools men and boys

The Management Committee meets regularly.

are not allowed to wear the five symbols, particularly the turban and the beard. Sometimes it can be women who are not allowed to wear Indian dress at work.

There are five staff who are paid and these include the two granthis, a Community Development Officer, a secretary and a full time caretaker. The two granthis look after the religious interests. The Community Development Officer is responsible for educational activities and for starting small clubs or groups where people can take part in activities of common interest.

MONEY

Woolwich Gurdwara depends on voluntary contributions for its income. The money is used for the upkeep of the Gurdwara and to pay wages to the two granthis and the caretaker. Some of the money is also spent in improving the building. Often members of the congregation give generous sums of money to the treasurer. To give you an example, when the kitchen was renovated and fitted with modern equipment and the new washing-

A member receiving material for a turban for service to the community.

up room was built, some people donated over a hundred pounds each.

From time to time important speakers visit the Gurdwara. They are normally presented with turbans which are also bought from the Gurdwara funds. Presenting a turban to a speaker or to any other person who might have done selfless service to the community, is regarded with great honour because a turban to the Sikhs is like a crown on the head.

COMMUNITY DEVELOPMENT OFFICE

In late 1977 the Ramgarhia Community Centre was successful in securing a grant to open a Community Development Office. This is the first known Gurdwara in England to have a full time Community Development Officer. Any person living in Woolwich can use the services of the Community Development Officer. He has to work in co-operation with the Management Committee and also let the local council know of his progress. The Woolwich Gurdwara through this office have been able to introduce many activities.

SENIOR CITIZENS CLUB

The main purpose of this club is to help the elderly Sikhs who are lonely at home, especially during the day time when their families are at work. The Club is open five days a week and the elderly meet, talk and share their views in Punjabi, read Punjabi newspapers, magazines and books. This keeps them occupied. They also help to do any tasks needing to be done in the Gurdwara. They learn English two days a week. They realise that it is important to learn English so that they can go about their daily lives when the family is away at work. Sometimes tours to different parts of England are arranged for them.

LANGUAGE CLASSES

English and Punjabi are the two languages taught at the Gurdwara. The English classes are mostly attended by women who are unable to speak the language. They learn to read and write but their main concern is to be able to speak and understand English. Most men, except the very elderly, know the language. Sikhs feel that both parents must know English so that they can

Both English and Punjabi are taught at the gurdwara.

A solicitor gives advice on legal matters.

take equal interest in their children's education, and social welfare. They also want to learn English so that they can take full part in the activities of Woolwich.

Sikh children in Britain grow up learning English in schools and Punjabi at home. The Punjabi they speak is often full of English words. As these children do not get any chance to learn Gurmukhi at school or at home, they learn it at the Gurdwara. Most Sikh parents take an interest in this scheme and send their children to the Gurdwara to learn Gurmukhi, so that they will not forget their traditions and their culture. These language classes are held in the evenings.

LEGAL ADVICE

The Management Committee of the Woolwich Gurdwara felt that the local Sikh community needed advice from time to time on various legal matters. Therefore, once a month in the evening, legal advice sessions are held free of charge at the Gurdwara by an Asian solicitor. Legal language is difficult enough to understand but it becomes even more difficult when English is not your language. It was decided to have an Asian solicitor because he would understand the legal difficulties of the people concerned and also be able to explain the laws to them in Punjabi.

WOMEN'S GROUP

In most activities men and women take part together, but here at Woolwich women have formed a successful group of their own. They meet once a week in the afternoon for prayer. They have their own small committee which organises various activities for the women. This group practises singing hymns for the gurpurbs or for the Sunday evening services. They are able to help the young people to learn those hymns.

Once a week a senior social worker from the local Council (a Punjabi woman) comes to the Gurdwara. Once again the reason for having a Punjabi speaking person is to help women to discuss any of their difficulties in a language they speak and understand. The social worker spends two hours with the women, who can ask her advice on matters such as children's education, family and household problems, pension schemes, social security benefits and any other matters that cause difficulties.

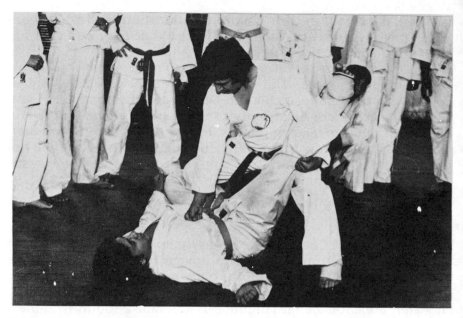

Youngsters play games and sports at the Youth Centre, while others enjoy reading books and magazines in the library.

SIKH YOUTH CENTRE

The Ramgarhia Assocation of the Woolwich Gurdwara has bought a separate building near the Gurdwara which they want to develop into an independent Youth Centre. Once this Centre is ready all the youth activities will move into that building, but at present the Youth Centre operates from the Woolwich Gurdwara.

Sikh children as well as children of other local residents take part in the Youth Centre activities. They play indoor games such as badminton, table tennis and billiards. Over a hundred youngsters learn karate and judo, a favourite sport among the boys. The Youth Centre has flourishing hockey and football teams.

These teams organise matches against other local teams. In fact the Centre's hockey team won the 1977/8 and 1978/9 championships for indoor hockey, in the Borough of Greenwich.

LIBRARY

The Library at the Gurdwara is well stocked with books. Here you can get books in Gurmukhi and English, about the lives of Sikh Gurus, Sikh history and culture, as well as story books for children and adults. Magazines, journals and newspapers again in English and Gurmukhi, printed locally and abroad, are also available in the Library. Anyone is welcome to use this library. At present the library opens for two hours twice a week. It is hoped that in the future the library will be open more often.

Over to you!

8. Over to you

This book has given you a glimpse into the life-style of Sikhs who have settled in a particular part of London. The religious life of the Sikhs is much the same all over the world, but their living conditions have changed according to the different environments. This happens with most people in the world who decide to live in a country other than their own. As immigrants, the Sikhs have brought with them customs, traditions and a way of life which is very different from the British way of life. Sikhs, who have come to settle here have also brought with them various skills, which they are contributing to British society. They also have difficulties. Many of their difficulties are similar to those of the British people but they are aggravated for the Sikhs because they are immigrants. This book may have helped you to understand why the Sikhs look different and have a different way of life. The important thing is that people of all religions and of different life styles should respect one another. Do you agree?

This book has not given you much of the historical background of the Sikhs. You can find out more about the history, religion and other practices of the Sikhs by reading other books. You can also write to the following addresses for further information.

1. Sikh Temple,
   Ramgarhia Association,
   Ramgarhia Community Centre,
   Masons Hill, Woolwich,
   London SE18 6EJ.

2. The Sikh Missionary Society (UK) Regd.
   10 Featherstone Road,
   Southall,
   Middlesex UB2 5AA.
   This society has produced about seventeen books in English on various aspects of Sikhism. You can get these books free by writing to the above address. The society also arranges lectures on Sikhism.

3. The Sikh Students Federation,
   10 Featherstone Road,
   Southall,
   Middlesex UB2 5AA.

This Federation was formed in 1955 by young Sikh Students studying at Universities and Colleges in Britain. They now have branches all over the country. They also publish and distribute literature on Sikhism, and run a library service. The members of the Federation will be very willing to come and talk to you about Sikh religion and its practices if you ask them.

Book List

Anne Farncombe, *Our Sikh Friends*, Denholm House Press – facts about Sikhs and their way of life, illustrated.

W. O. Cole and Piara Singh Sambhi, *Sikhism*, Ward Lock – covers Sikh beliefs and practices, for 13 years upwards, illustrated.

W. O. Cole, *A Sikh Family in Britain*, Pergamon – describes the Sikh way of life in Britain and their rites, 10–15 year olds.

W. H. McLeod, *The Way of the Sikh*, Hulton – Sikh history for 11–14 year olds.

Stories from Sikh History (8 volumes), Hemkunt Press, New Delhi – Sikh history and its development, a useful source book.

Sean Lyle, *Pavan is a Sikh*, A. & C. Black – describes a boy and his family living in London, for 9 years upwards.

Piara Singh Sambhi, *Understanding Your Sikh Neighbour*, Lutterworth – meeting a Sikh family in Britain, for 11 years upwards, illustrated.

W. O. Cole, *Thinking About Sikhism*, Lutterworth – Sikh history and beliefs for 15 years upwards, illustrated.

Glossary

Achkan, a tailored knee length top.

Akhand Path, continuous reading of the Granth Sahib completed in 48 hours.

Amrit, baptismal water.

Amrit Parchar, initiation ceremony.

Anand Sahib, hymns of joy.

Ardas, a special Sikh prayer.

Baisakhi, festival to mark the Sikh new year.

Chakkar, a circle as seen in the Sikh sign (see notes on the Sikh flag).

Chanani, a canopy made of cloth over the Granth Sahib.

Chaur, Yak hair embedded in a wooden or silver handle used for waving over the Granth Sahib. Also called Chauri.

Churidar Pyjamas, tight fitting pair of Indian trousers.

Dhoti, cloth tied round the waist downwards in a special manner.

Dupatta/Chuni, a scarf worn by women.

Giani, a scholar of Punjabi language and literature.

Granth Sahib, the Sikh Holy Book.

Granthi, a man who looks after the Granth Sahib.

Gurbani, the writings of the Gurus in the Granth Sahib.

Gurdwara, Sikh place of worship.

Gurpurb, Sikh festival.

Guru, a religious teacher. Also used before the names of the ten Sikh Gurus, or of the Guru Granth Sahib.

Guru ka Langar, food cooked in the community kitchen of a gurdwara.

Hukamnamah/Vak, random reading taken from the Guru Granth Sahib.

Japji Sahib, morning prayer.

Kameeze, knee length dress worn over Indian trousers by women.

Khalsa, the pure ones/baptised Sikhs.

Khanda, Sikh sign. Also the double edged sword.

Kirtan Sohilla, night prayer. Song of praise.

Kurta, loose top worn by men and women over tight Indian trousers.

Lavan, the wedding song.
Manji Sahib, small bed on which Granth Sahib is placed.
Mool Mantra, Guru Nanak's description of God.
Nishan Sahib, Sikh flag.
Panj Pyare, the Five Beloved.
Patasas, puffed sugar cakes (no English word to give proper description).
Patka, squared piece of cloth to cover the long hair of boys.
Rehras, evening prayer.
Rumala, a cloth covering over Granth Sahib.
Salwar (Shalwar), specially designed loose Indian trousers for women.
Sehaj Path, slow reading of Granth Sahib.

Index